Adunah*

by

ARAME RICHARDSON

IØWI

Adunah*
* *Adunah is the Wolof word for 'world' 'universe'*

© 2019 Arame Richardson
All Rights Reserved.

Cover image:
Shutterstock.com

Author Photo:
Arame Richardson

Design & Layout
In Our Words Inc.
inourwords.ca

ISBN: 978-1-989403-05-1

No part of this publication may be reproduced, stored in a retrieval system or transmited in any form or by any means, elecronic, mechanical, photocopying, recording, scanning or otherwise, except with the prior written permission from the author, except for brief quotes/passage for review purposes.

Dedication

to my mother

Acknowledgements

My deepest gratitude
to my family, friends, collaborators,
Caramel and Smittens,
to my teachers and professors.
Without all of you,
my *adunah* would not have evolved
into what it is today.
I love you all.

Contents

The Immigrants 1

- *Privilège des immigrants*.................. 2
- Immigrant's child........................... 4
- My friend's Sunday blues................. 5
- Beggars.. 6
- Hunger... 7
- *Nulle part* Nowhere........................ 9

Mother Daughter 11

- *Jamais*.. 12
- My mother................................... 13
- My daughter................................. 16
- My mother................................... 17
- My daughter................................. 19
- 2 am.. 20
- Don't judge me............................. 21
- *Adunah!*..................................... 22
- Paris without a smile..................... 24
- Trains.. 25
- Loose cigarettes............................ 26

Colonization & Politics 27

1884	28
Roots	29
1961	30
1987	31
You need me	32
Privilege	33
Generosity	34
The looks	35
I see my people	36
Arcadia	38
Beautiful children	39
Love	40
Forgiveness	41
Long rides	42
Work	43
Lagos City	44
Que faire?	47
Gimmicks	48
Under the shadows	50
Out of site	51
Sunshine child!	52

Faith 53

Faith	54
The court	55

Believe in yourself.. 56
The uncertainties of life............................. 57
The tree.. 58
Strange land... 59
Public schools.. 60
Dream.. 61
Hope.. 63

The Pink Revolver   *64*

The Immigrants

Privilège des immigrants

Yesterday
I picked her up
She spoke Spanish
She spoke English

Her mother and her aunt spoke only Spanish
They asked her
¿No es caro esto?
Cogiendo Uber
¿Todos los días?

She said
Esto es uno de los pequeños privilegios
Que tenemos aquí
En los Estados Unidos
¡Además! no es caro

Today
I am here
At Prince Georges County
Getting a pedicure
I am relaxing
I am writing a poem

I spent seven hours dealing with
Technicians
They could not help me
Though they tried
My new computer refused to download
The Adobe software
I went to the library
Still no help
¡Que Coñaso!

My pedicure is one of the few
Privileges that I have
I love my Vietnamese friends
They always smile
They do their work
They collect their money
They speak their language
They say thank you

Their privilege
They go to the casino every Sunday

Immigrant's child

You are
Big
Grown
Beautiful
Educated
Hybrid

You are because I am
The immigrant
The poor
The single mother

You are because I am
The foreigner
The pariah
The misfit

Unfortunately for me
Fortunately for you
You are because I am

My friend's Sunday blues

People are in church
Others are sleeping
I am just sitting here

On my couch
My head is tilted
The flow

Everything I ever own
Has been taken away from me

Gone

Sunday Blues!

Nature
Trees
Flowers
Pawns
Chirp
Quack

My Sunday
My walk
My nature

Beggars

You always beg for my love
I always beg for a ring
You continue to beg for my loving
I continue to beg for a legal companion
We are all beggars

Like the little boys on the streets of Dakar
The addicts on the street of Baltimore
The Indian women and their children in
Parisian metro
We are all beggars

You said
"my mother said, beggars don't choose"
Why are you choosing
Why are you begging

Four years later
You are still begging
I am still begging

We are all beggars
Not everyone
Gives

Hunger

The world is hungry
The students are hungry
The neighbors are hungry
We're all hungry

I ate my lunch
I am still hungry

Shrimp egg roll!

The corner-store
Two shrimp egg rolls
Jesus!
I can't
Salty
Nasty
I can't pass the first bite
Salty
I cut it open

Just salt
Lots of salt
Cabbage
Just cabbage
Stale

No shrimp
Old
Stale again!

Ouch!
Stop killing my people
Stop cheating
Stop stealing
Stop being selfish
Stop being mean
Just go home!

Nulle part
Nowhere

I am here
Je suis là
Je dois foutre le camp
I gotta go
Où
Where
I don't have a home
Je n'ai plus un chez moi
J'en ai marre
I am fed up

Mother Daughter

Jamais

Never
When I was little
My mother used to say
"il ne faut jamais dire fontaine …"
Never say never
Who would have thought …

My mother

When I was little
I did not like my mother
My mother did not like me
I loved my grandmother
My grandmother loved me

My mother she hated me
She hit me
She punched me

She hit me
With
The belt
The shoe
The stick
When she sewed my clothes
I tried the clothes
I moved
She stuck a needle in
My arm
My back

Ouch!
You're mean!
Why

She hated me
She loved my sister
She loved everyone
She hated me

When I grew up
I turned fifteen

She hit me
I hit her back
She hit me again
Then she slapped me
Then I slapped her back

She throws me on the ground
Then I throw her on the ground

Daddy came
Stop hitting her!
She will never let you hit her again!

When I got older
I left her
I left her house
I left her compound
I left her country
I stayed gone

No more pain
No more questions
No more misery

Today
I love her
I forgive her
No more pain

My daughter

"Mom! Stop travelling!
So you can save money!"
So I can inherit
So I can enjoy what I did not work for
Ouch!

I know I am sorry
I am trying
I can see you
I can hear you
But I also need to travel

That's where I live
Traveling is my comfort zone
I no longer have a home

The dreams
The universe
The smell of new area
The slow walk while observing

My travels
My wellbeing
My peace of mind

My mother

I don't see you
I miss you
I have not seen you in five years
I know
It breaks my heart

I look at people with their mothers
They walk around
They do errands together
They cook together
They eat together

Me, I just stare
I just look at them
I stare in the empty

Deep inside the emptiness
I see you
I wish I could fly to see you ever so often
But I cannot

I have to work
I became a slave
A self-made slave

I stare in the empty when I am depressed
I wish I could run to you

So I just pick up the phone
I use Viber
Years ago
I used Skype
When just a few people knew about Skype
The famous lady O talked about Skype on TV
That day she thought she did people a service
Maybe she did
But for me
That was the end
Everyone started using Skype

Me, I lost my only way of communication
with my mother
After that day
I just stare in the empty for years
Until finally one day I saw Whatsapp
Blessings!
My savior
My angel
My oxygen

My daughter

She said
I don't understand
How people open their legs
Make children and disappear
Ouch!

Be careful my daughter
Be careful about yourself
Be careful about your words

My late grandmother used to say
"Words are like bullets
Before you know it
They've already killed someone"

For many
The act of intimacy
Is a natural gift
A gift of the universe

For that my daughter
Be careful about your words

2 am

I can't sleep
I went to bed too early
Let me write
A poem

Don't judge me

It's not your place
I fed you
I rocked you
I sheltered you
I protected you

Don't judge me
I gave you more than
I could give you
And even more
Don't judge me

Adunah!

Who would have thought
there is no place like home

What is it like to leave my home
to claim someone else's home
that will never be my home

To them,
I am
The alien
The stranger
The one everyone beats in court

A constant struggle for
Space
Identity
Culture

When I go home
It's no longer my home
Thiey! Adunah!
Everything has changed
For the worst
Maybe for the best for some

I can no longer fit in
I am someone else

My new address is the universe
And everything that it offers except
A real home
Thiey! Adunah!

* *Adunah* means world/universe
** *Thiey* means gosh! [indicating surprise]

Paris without a smile

Stares without a smile
Uncomfortable
Indifferent
Fachos
No stares
Bleddards
Kilometers of stares

Trains

Man playing *accordéon*
Smooth sound
Captivating
No reactions
A couple of Euros
Foreign women
With child begging
Language
Culture
Starving
Dommage !

Loose cigarettes

Paris
2 am out of cigarettes
Le marchant du coin
Dakar
Loose cigarettes
All day
All night
United States
Loose cigarettes
The street
The police
Gardner
Dommage !

Colonization & Politics

Rescue me, O my God,
from the hand of the wicked,
from the grasp
of the unjust and cruel.
Psalm 71:4

1884

Berlin
Notre destin
Des siècles
À venir
1965
Colonized
1985
Still colonized
2018
Still colonized
Weak leaders
Greed
Try to stand on your own
Stop Neo-colonization
Enculés!!!!!!!!!!

Roots

I know it was hard
I know the journey was
Long and tumultuous
I am sorry for everything

I wish I could go back in time
To help
To heal
To protect
I should have been there

I can feel the remorse
I can feel the sadness
It's all right

I am sorry for everything
That you had to go through
I have been praying for the pain
I have been praying for the sorrows

1961

I was there
I knew him
He was great
Short lived dream

First recipe
Cobalt
Politics

I am a priest
J'ai prêté serment
Oh là la !
Pauvre con!
The promise
The grave
Patrice Lumumba

1987

I don't need your charity
I will make my own
Not allowed

See!
I told you
Not even five years
I did it

Not allowed
Neo-colonialism

The other
Not allowed
The best friend
The plot
The conspiracy

Boom !
No more
Now you need
Charity
Thomas Sankara

You need me

You are
Because
I am
I am your foundation
I am your mud
You need me
Without me your house will crumble
You need me

Privilege

People talk about
Privilege
It seems like a new word
Just like slavery
Privilege existed in all societies
Nowadays privilege is
In all walks of life
Where there is a majority
There is privilege
Where there is power
There is privilege
Dig deep
Go get your own privilege

Generosity

You are so generous
Yet what you take is hidden
What you give
Is publicized
You keep on taking
They keep on leaving
Have you thought about stopping?
Maybe they will stay

The looks

When they look at their own kind
They smile
They look at them with kindness
They admire them

When they look at me
Their eyes like swords
Lay on me
My soul
My heart

I still walk tall and noble
I am sorry if that's an offense

Deep inside me I say to myself
Evil heart
Evil spirit
Oops!
That's God's gift
I am sorry I don't have the power to heal your cancer
I wish I could heal your cancer

Every human being has a natural gift
That gives them the right to exist

I see my people

I am driving you around
You are smiling
You are happy
The places you go to
Are bright
Clean
Everybody is happy
Everyone is laughing

On the way to dropping you off
I see my people
In the dark
In dirty neighborhoods
No lights
I see my people
They are looking desperate

My heart is broken
I am broken
My brain is broken
I want to scream
I want to yell
I want to build for them
Nice houses
Nice restaurants

Nice neighborhoods

I want to get them a nice job
I want them to stay long on the job
I want them to make enough dough
So they can also

Smile like you
Be happy like you
Go to places like you

Places
where there are lights
like your neighborhood
where it is clean
Everybody is happy
Everyone is laughing
I see my people

Arcadia

Beautiful neighborhood
Beautiful trees
Streets so small
Full of beautiful cars

No bus stops
No liquor stores
No check cashing place
Who lives here?

Beautiful children

Beautiful smiles
Beautiful hearts

Everything taken away
From these children

Stop stealing from
These beautiful children

Love

Keep your heart open
Dwell in the house of humility
Smile and be generous
Trust yourself
When others may doubt
Love
And
Accept yourself

Forgiveness

A hard and long process
The hardest thing to do
but we must strive

Long rides

Taking trains
Riding as far as it can go
Riding and writing

You were lost, I help you
Language   Culture
We walk together we took
The car   Air France
We got on the same next train
This time I have to escort you to Charles De Gaulle Airport

Generosity
Would you have done the same for me
I came to your country

I got lost too
None look at me
None seem to care

Tropical weather
Just like my country
Street food just like
My place of birth
God showed me the way

Work

Be careful about yourself
Be careful about everything
Tiptoe around yourself
And around everything
Don't make any mistake

Though people will use your mistake
To walk all over you
Then get ahead of you

Dwell in uncertainty
It is your safe place

Lagos City

People told me
Don't go to Nigeria

And I said
I will go to Nigeria
Nigeria is also my home

I was born in Africa
I grew up in Africa
Why should I be afraid of Nigeria
Nigeria is inside Africa

I am here now
What I see in Nigeria

Peace
Love
Respect
Service
Corruption
Beggars
Chaos

I see these in all four continents
Now tell me

I hear
I hear welcome mam
Thank you mam
Good morning mam
Good afternoon mam
Happy Sunday mam

I see
Love
Appreciation
Service
Perfection

When was the last time someone said
Hello to me
Admired me
Contemplated me with kindness
Loved me
Served me
Good vegetable soup
Smiled at me

When was the last time
Someone showed me that I am visible

No eyes like swords
No angry looks

Instead
Infinite appreciation

Don't go to Nigeria
What?
Stop demonizing
You wish to go to Nigeria

Nigeria is
The land of humanity
The land of love
The land of respect
The land of shout
The land of chaos
Beautiful chaos!

But don't drive in Nigeria
It's "Nigerious"

Que faire ?

Des batoubas aux regards aiguisés
Qui se battent sans arrêt pour
Bloquer l'entrée du jardin

Des takahas aux regards farouches
Qui se battent sans arrêt pour
Entrer dans le jardin

Des étrangers qui se trouvent
Coincés entre deux mondes
Deux mondes pleins de haine
Et de rancœur

La place des étrangers
Est très ambiguë
Jamais imaginé
Autant de rancœur

Que faire ?

Gimmicks

My school
Your lies
Our gimmicks

Get your associate degree
You'll make more money
Gimmick
Get you Bachelor's degree
You'll make more money
Gimmick

Get your Master's
You'll get a better job
Gimmick

Where is my money
Where is my job
Gimmick

Let me go
Just let me go
I have to get mine

I wish Daddy showed me
How to get my own

No worry!
I am learning
On my own
How to get my own

Under the shadows

I will shut it off
What
You can't do that
Watch me

The wall
The border
The "outsiders"
The hard-workers
The contributors

The economic refugees
The political refugees
The violence refugees

Give me a taco
Give me a Margherita
I can't breathe
I need a shot of Cuervo

Out of site

The phone rang
Allo!
Bonjour!
Nanga deff?
Mangi fi rekk!
Haha!

Your president just gave us millions of dollars!
How nice!
I said: "how much did he take under the shadow?"

She kept silent
No more laughter
I used to think like you mom!

No more
Silence
Oops!

Sunshine child!

The sunshine child
smiles everyday
After entering the bright window
the sunshine
caresses your cheek
it makes you smile
Smile sunshine child

Faith

**Faith is confidence
in what we hope for
and assurance about what
we do not see.
Hebrew 11:1 NIV**

Faith

In the depth of your being
resides faith
it's yours
use it

The court

They live in my house
They don't pay rent
They took my furniture
They destroy my appliances
When I was going to court
The cab driver said
They own the court
I lost everything
Except my Faith

Believe in yourself

In a moment of darkness
Sorrow
Plots
Self-doubt
Believe in the depth of
Your inner beauty
Your kindness
Your soul

The uncertainties of life

sometimes in life
when we least expect it
a hurricane comes by and destroys everything
a hurricane is
of course
caused by
selfishness
humans disrespecting
other human beings
a hurricane is life's creation
they destroy
demean and reduce to nothing
a hurricane does not discriminate
you just have to be there when it hits
it is a natural disaster

The tree

I know I hung on
that windy tree
that wanted and unwanted tree
swung there for twenty-three long years

bounded by that same
wounded wait time
and desperation

wounded by sorrow
none gave me bread
none gave me drink

Strange land

In the moonlight
I met Chêne
From a strange light
Chêne smiles

Deep in the Cave
The moonlight
Shines
Chêne smiles

And why are you
Smiling
Deep in the dark
I see light
You see dark

I knew
Chêne knew better

Public schools

I hear loud students
I hear songs from students
I hear profanities

I feel disrespected
I feel nothing
I feel numb
I feel mocked
I feel stared

I notice a scent, a different smell
Sweat
Dirt
Clean
Dust

Spacious room
Bright light coming from the large windows
Cool air coming from the AC
Dirty vents
Dirty windows

No motivation
Just obligation
Just frustration
How can we help

Dream

What did I dream about last night
I dreamed of nothing
I have no dreams
I was just too tired to dream
But my friend told me
He could not sleep
When I asked why

He said
You snored
All night long
I could not close my eyes

But I know better
He was more frustrated
Actually, he thought things would go his way
Since it did not
He has to find an excuse

I no longer trust them
If they chose to sleep in the same
Bed for hope that something will happen
Too bad
Those days are gone
I enjoy my celibacy

My late grandmother used to say
People who wake up before you do
Will tell you to cover your butt
Meaning you were uncovered while sleeping

Where in fact they also were uncovered
While sleeping
Meaning their butt was also out

On the following day
the same person who said he could not sleep
because of my snores
falls asleep before me and was snoring so loud
that I could not even sleep

Hope
Inspired by Psalm 71:5

I was lonely
But I have hope

My children left for college
Just me in the house
But I have hope

At work
I was a pariah
But I have hope

My male friend
Suffers from the vestiges of slavery
Nothing I could do about it
But I have hope

I wanted to go back to my home
Where I am a queen
Where I am not a pariah
But I thought about my daughters
So I stay here
I have hope

I breathe hope
I eat hope
Hope keeps me breathing
I am grateful to have hope

The Pink Revolver
A True Story

TITLE CARD 1.
GUN SHOP. MORNING, 11 AM

Two months after her home invasion, MARIETOU, a 5'5" medium-built woman, enters a gun shop where three men stand behind the counter. One of the three men, the older one with a pot belly and a salt and pepper beard smiles and walks toward her. He wears overwashed blue jeans with red suspenders and an old white shirt with yellow sweat stains in the armpits. MARIETOU's confidence fades as she looks at the display of all kinds of guns and hunting material such as knives, rifles and gas spray. She looks nervous and out of her element.

INTERIOR OF GUN SHOP

GUN SHOP OWNER: Can I help you, young lady?
MARIETOU *(stuttering, in a thick accent, points to a gun in the display cabinet)*: Uh... I want to buy a...
GUN SHOP OWNER: Let me guess, a gun? You're at the right place!

MARIETOU: Yes. Okay.
GUN SHOP OWNER: What kind of gun do you want? Do you want an automatic or semi-automatic; a shot gun or a revolver?
MARIETOU: I don't know, let me look first. What do you have?
GUN SHOP OWNER: All kinds of guns, you name it.
MARIETOU *(mistakes the shot gun and the short gun):* Let me see the 'short gun.'
GUN SHOP OWNER: This is a shot gun, it's fast and easy, my mother owns one.
MARIETOU: Whoa! This cannot possibly be a short gun, it's too long.
Gun Shop Owner chuckles and demonstrates how to use the shot gun and where to hide it.
MARIETOU: No, I want something smaller, something easy to hide. What about a Beretta? I heard a lot about Berettas.
GUN SHOP OWNER: Yes, that's a nice one and it's small.
The Gun Shop Owner shows MARIETOU the Beretta and demonstrates how it works. MARIETOU tries it herself. She pulls the safety clip and tries to repeat what the owner just did and screams as it clips her thumb in the process.
MARIETOU: Ouch! That hurts! I can't do it!

GUN SHOP OWNER: Yes, you can. Here watch me, and try it again.
MARIETOU gets frustrated as she cannot get the gun to open the second time.
MARIETOU: No, I pass. Let's look for something else. What about this pink revolver right here? It looks small.
GUN SHOP OWNER: Yep, they call it a woman's gun, probably because it is pink and small. It is also easy to operate, just open, load and shoot.
MARIETOU tries and confirms the three easy steps.
MARIETOU: That's it! I'll take it.

CUT TO TITLE CARD 2: 'LIFE BEFORE THE ROBBERY'

INTERIOR OF APARTMENT. 9 PM
MARIETOU walks into her house, goes straight to her room and locks the door behind her. She is holding the pink revolver and a cartridge of 38-millimeter bullets.

CUT TO TITLE CARD 3:
INSERT FLASHBACK: MARIETOU's hand holding the gun, thinking.

We see MARIETOU go through her nightly routine. She gets undressed, takes a shower, walks to the kitchen to fix a plate of dinner and then feeds her babies. She watches TV for a while and then everybody goes to bed at ten o'clock.

CUT TO TITLE CARD 4: THE NIGHT OF THE ROBBERY 4 AM

The babies' cries are loud. At the same time, the bedroom door opens, someone switches the light on and MARIETOU sees a man, an intruder, standing in the doorway. MARIETOU is startled and shaking.

INTRUDER *(in a deep voice):* Where is the money? Do you have any drugs here?

MARIETOU: No, I don't have any money and I don't have any drugs. I just moved here.

(wide angle)

The bedroom door shuts again while "deep voice" is talking to someone in the living room of the apartment. While they are still talking MARIETOU takes the opportunity to grab the phone and dials 911 with trembling fingers, still lying down.

911 OPERATOR (OC): Ma'am, what's your address?

MARIETOU: 315 Park Ave.

911 OPERATOR (OC): What's your name?
MARIETOU stops and stares as two intruders enter the bedroom. Close up shot of the first intruder.
INTRUDER *(in an angry voice):* Oh, you can call the police, we will be gone by the time they get here.

The bedroom door shuts again and there is a long silence. MARIETOU finally gets out of bed, trembling. She opens the bedroom door and heads to the living room. She opens her purse to check her wallet. It was empty. She runs into the kitchen where the two intruders are eating.

MARIETOU: Where is my rent money? Give it back to me. Eating my food too? Do you want me to cook for you, too? Fils de pute, sales Américains.
INTRUDER: What's that? Is that some kinda food? English please. English.
MARIETOU: Va te faire enculer. Américains de merde. Rends-moi mon argent, imbécile.
SECOND INTRUDER: Man, let's get the fuck outta here, au revoir mademoiselle.
MARIETOU: Enculés !

The intruders hear the far-off sirens and leave through the same window they entered. MARIETOU goes to her bedroom to check on the crying babies. She walks to the door carrying one crying baby. We hear loud knocks on the door and she lets the police officers in.

CUT TO TITLE CARD 5. THE BIG DOGS

FADE IN: INTERIOR OF MARIETOU'S HOUSE 4:45 AM

We hear loud knocks. MARIETOU rushes to open the door. Four burly police officers walk in authoritatively, with hands on their guns and radios beeping. They follow MARIETOU to the empty living room which has a TV in one corner and a red couch opposite it. She faces the officers.

MARIETOU (in a panicked voice): I've been robbed. It was two men. They just left through that window. They broke the glass and came in from there.

OFFICER ONE: How long ago?

MARIETOU: Just now, they left when they heard your siren.

OFFICER TWO: Describe them. What race?

MARIETOU: Two black guys. One with

lighter-skin, the other brown-skinned.
OFFICER ONE: How tall? How big?
MARIETOU: One was medium-built, the other, the brown skin one was slim built. They took my money. They ate my sandwich that I was saving for my breakfast. They ate my cookies. One of them had the nerve to say 'au revoir mademoiselle.'

MARIETOU walks to the window to show the officers where the robbers had entered. The officers approached.

OFFICER ONE *(speaks into his shoulder radio and exits the room)*: Home invasion, two black males, one heavy-built …

Officer One returns holding a black suitcase. Officer three notices some visible fingerprints on the microwave.

OFFICER THREE *(in an amused voice)*: Whoa, these guys are really bold. And stupid. They warm up food, eat your sandwich and cookies and leave their prints all over the place.

OFFICER FOUR: You say you did not hear anything?

MARIETOU *(pointing towards her bedroom)*: My bedroom is all the way at the back of the apartment and the door was shut. I always shut it.

OFFICER TWO *(pointing to the security locks):* Wow, young lady, either you sleep deep or they really didn't make any noise.

At this point MARIETOU looks confused and upset at the same time. The officer with the kit starts to spread black powder on the microwave, the window and other places and brushes it off for fingerprints. The officers go to one side and speak quietly. MARIETOU could not hear.

MARIETOU *(looking confused and angry):* That's it? Now what? You guys are worse than the police in Senegal. Over there, the police shows up hours and hours after a crime. Most of the time we have to catch the bandits ourselves and take them to the station. Here in America, you have fast cars, sirens, and pistols and you don't bother to even chase the thieves. What am I supposed to do with fingerprints?

OFFICER ONE *(smirking):* Oh well, Ma'am, feel free to go chase after them.

OFFICER TWO *(with a smirk):* We will let you know if we find them. We'll be in touch.

After 10 minutes the officers left with their notepads.

CUT TO TITLE CARD 7: PHONE CONVERSATION WITH SADY

In Wolof, mixed with French and English, we hear MARIETOU telling SADY about the robbery.

MARIETOU *(to SADY)*: Ask your wife if I can stay with you until I figure out what to do next. Please come pick me up now. I can't no longer stay here.

We see MARIETOU pack two suitcases of clothes and leave everything else in the apartment.

CUT TO SADY'S HOUSE INTERIOR
FADE IN: *We see SADY and his wife sitting next to each other and MARIETOU with her two babies in their car seats.*

CUT TO TITLE CARD 8: SLEEPLESS NIGHT 10 PM
INSERT FLASHBACK: MARIETOU tossing and turning
We see MARIETOU toss and turn, unable to sleep. After an hour, she turns the light on and grabs her book Chief of Station, Congo *by Larry Delvin and reads. She stops after a long*

while, rubbing her eyes, yet still awake. Montage of MARIETOU staring at the clock at 1 AM, then 3 AM then finally at 6 AM. The morning light floods the room as her babies sit for their first feed.
She is seen cooking and eating in front of the TV. She picks up the phone and calls her girlfriend D'NIA. D'NIA is a 5'4" slim, African-American, 25 years old with dark, wavy hair. They talk.

CUT TO TITLE CARD 9: I SAW HIM AGAIN, PARK AVE 6 PM

We see MARIETOU holding grocery bags, crossing a street in her old neighborhood. We see a young man sitting on the corner a few meters away.

MARIETOU walks in his direction, puts down her grocery bags and starts to dial D'NIA's number.

MARIETOU *(on phone):* Hey girl!

D'NIA *(on phone):* Hey what's up?

MARIETOU: Guess what? I just came from my old neighborhood and I saw one of the guys, the thieves, who came to my place.

D'NIA: Nooo, what? Again? Poor girl! What did you do?

MARIETOU: The same thing I did the first time I saw him. I stopped a half block away and called the cops. Twice I called them. You know how that goes. I waited for half an hour and they never showed up. The bastardo left ten minutes after I called. I got tired of waiting and left too.
D'NIA: Oh Gosh! Just take it easy, it's gonna be all right.
MARIETOU: Stop telling me take it easy! It didn't happen to you. You go to sleep every night after you turn your lights off. Me, I have to toss and turn, read and reread, put the light on and off. I am tired, I am exhausted. I got to find a way to find some sleep. You know what? I will make this right. I am going to buy a gun.
D'NIA: No! Don't do that. I can go with you to a therapist who will help you calm down and sleep. It takes time to get over something like this. You will forget and put all this behind you. Getting a gun is just crazy. Out here, only thugs and cops own guns and of course crazy people. You're gonna walk around with a gun like a thug? If you get caught, you're going to jail. And if you shoot someone, you are never coming out again.

MARIETOU *(on phone):* Better to be on the bench as the defendant than to be in a casket. OK I have to go now. I'll call you later.
D'NIA *(on phone):* Wait, Marietou! Don't do anything crazy. Hello... Hello... oh hell, that girl's gone crazy.

CUT TO TITLE CARD 10: D'NIA VISITS MARIETOU AT SADY'S HOUSE

Scene opens with the sound of a doorbell. Sady's wife Mali opens the door and lets D'NIA into the house/room. Now all four (MARIETOU, SADY, MALI and D'NIA) are sitting in the living room talking.

D'NIA TO MARIETOU: How long do you think you will stay here?
Before Marietou can say anything, Mali says.
MALI: Oh! She can stay as long as she wants. Or until she finds another apartment.
MARIETOU *(in a thoughtful voice)*: I just don't know. Where do I go? What do I do next? I can't stay here forever. I don't want to be a burden to you.
SADY: She is just shook up now. She needs some time to rest. Everything will be all right. Give it some time.

MARIETOU *(sounding frustrated)*: Give what some time? I am buying a gun. Next time thieves come to my house; I'll shoot. I swear.
D'NIA: Girl, stop. You were really serious over the phone. Buying a gun? You kidding me, right? Now you really gone crazy, girl.
MARIETOU walks around the apartment gathering her stuff. She grabs her purse and her keys.

CUT TO TITLE CARD 11: GOING AFTER HIM TWO AND HALF YEARS LATER

On the street in MARIETOU's old neighborhood 9pm
MARIETOU is obviously on her way home from work. She is wearing a brightly-printed nurse's scrubs with white shoes. She has a crossover shoulder purse and is browsing a wayside African market on Park Ave. She comes out with a bag of groceries. Suddenly she stops and stares at someone who is sitting on the steps of a closed store drinking from a beer bottle wrapped in a paper bag. MARIETOU walks straight toward him. The man gets up and starts walking away from her, first slow, then faster and faster. We see MARIETOU drop her grocery bags and follow the man with her hand in her purse, the man

starts to run and MARIETOU runs after him. Both MARIETOU and the guy find themselves in a dark alley. We hear two gunshots.

FADE IN
INSIDE MARIETOU'S HOUSE 10 PM
We see MARIETOU in her apartment with the 'intruder' who is limping and there is blood dripping down his leg. He looks like he is in great pain and is very upset. MARIETOU is busy helping him with his leg wound; they start talking.

INTRUDER: What the hell am I doing in your damn apartment! I need to go to the hospital.

MARIETOU: Oh! You're fine. The bullet just grazed you. I can stop the bleeding and bandage it. I am a nurse. I can help you. I do this every day.

INTRUDER: Oh yeah, right! You're a nurse going off on a shooting spree every day. I should go to the hospital or the police and get your nurse ass in trouble.

MARIETOU: You cost me two and half years of sleep deprivation. This minor injury is nothing compared to what I go through every night.

INTRUDER: You just need to loosen up. You need some man company. Someone to hold you tight at night, so you can feel safe. You'll sleep like a baby. What's your name?
MARIETOU *(hesitant)*: Marietou.
INTRUDER: I'm James. James McNight.
Marietou didn't say anything. She proceeds with the treatment gently. She gave him a pill for the pain.
MARIETOU *(softly)*: Take it. It's a painkiller. You should be fine in a couple of hours.

We see MARIETOU lying down to sleep on her bed. James sleeps on the couch.

FADE IN:
CUT TO TITLE CARD 11: MARIETOU CUDDLING WITH JAMES

INSIDE MARIETOU'S APARTMENT. HOURS LATER
We see Marietou and James cuddling in spoon position in MARIETOU's bed, not saying a word.

THE END

Other books by
Arame Richardson:

The Immigrants' Chronicles

www.ingramcontent.com/pod-product-compliance
Lightning Source LLC
Chambersburg PA
CBHW020546080526
44583CB00013B/1014